The Wild Life of BEARS

By Camilla de la Bédoyère

WINDMILL BOOKS

THE WILD SIDE

Published in 2015 by **WINDMILL BOOKS**, an Imprint of Rosen Publishing
29 East 21st Street, New York, NY 10010

Publishing Director: Belinda Gallagher
Creative Director: Jo Cowan
Editorial Director: Rosie McGuire
Editor: Sarah Parkin
Designers: Jo Cowan, Joe Jones
Image Manager: Liberty Newton
Production Manager: Elizabeth Collins
Reprographics: Stephan Davis, Anthony Cambray, Jennifer Cozens

ACKNOWLEDGEMENTS

The publishers would like to thank Mike Foster (Maltings Partnership), Joe Jones, and Richard Watson (Bright Agency) for
the illustrations they contributed to this book. All other artwork from the Miles Kelly Artwork Bank.

The publishers would like to thank the following sources for the use of their photographs: t = top, b = bottom, l = left,
r = right, c = center, bg = background, rt = repeated throughout. **Cover** (front) Hung Chung Chih/Shutterstock; (back) Ilya
Akinshin, (Speech panel) Tropinina Olga. **Alamy** 18 Arco Images GmbH. **Dreamstime** 5(giant panda) Hungchungchih,
(sloth bear) Mvshiv, (moon bear) Karelgallas, (American black bear) Hilbell; 7(t) Petrmasek. **FLPA** 10 Jules Cox; 12 Theo
Allofs/ Minden Pictures; 13(t) Jules Cox; 14 Katherine Feng/Minden Pictures; 15(b) Jules Cox; 19(t) Matthias Breiter/Minden
Pictures, (b) Terry Whittaker. **Fotolia** 8–9(bg) bluesky; 16–17(bg) Kirsty Pargeter. **Nature Picture Library** 15(t) Axel
Gomille. **Photo Discs/Digital Stock** 5(brown bear). **Photo Discs/ImageState** Heading panel(rt). **Shutterstock**
Joke panel(rt) Tropinina Olga; Learn a Word panel(rt) donatas1205; 1 Hung Chung Chih 3 Eric Isselée; 4–5 Ilya Akinshin;
5(sun bear) Cuson, (spectacled bear) Matt Hart; 6 Richard Seeley; 7(b) Khoroshunova Olga; 8(brush stroke tl) Ambient Ideas;
9(paint splatter tl) sabri deniz kizil, (l) Anna Ts, (br) jennipenni89; 11(b) Antoine Beyeler; 13(r) Marcin Niemiec; 16(paper tl)
sharpner, (berries tl) Andra Popovici, (panda panel tr) jennipenni89, (b) donatas1205, (bear b) VectorZilla; 17(paper cl) House
@ Brasil Art Studio, (bl) MisterElements; 20–21 Dennis Donohue; 21(r) Uryadnikov Sergey.

LIBRARY OF CONGRESS CATALOGING-IN-PUBLICATION DATA

De la Bédoyère, Camilla, author.
 The wild life of bears / Camilla de la Bedoyere.
     pages cm. — (The wild side)
 Includes index.
 ISBN 978-1-4777-5515-0 (pbk.)
 ISBN 978-1-4777-5516-7 (6 pack)
 ISBN 978-1-4777-5514-3 (library binding)
 1. Bears—Juvenile literature. I. Title.
 QL737.C27D448 2015
 599.78—dc23
                                    2014027099

Manufactured in the United States of America

CPSIA Compliance Information: Batch #CW15WM: For Further Information contact Rosen Publishing, New York, New York at 1-800-237-9932

Contents

I am a bear!

I am a kind of animal called a mammal. Mammals have warm blood, fur or hair, and we feed our babies on milk.

Powerful shoulders

Big snout

Small eyes

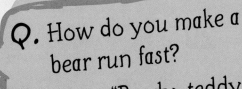

Q. How do you make a bear run fast?

A. Shout, "Ready, teddy, go!"

Four strong legs

4

Thick, furry coat

Polar bear

Large paws

Types of bear

There are eight types of bear and most of them live in forests.

Brown bear

Giant panda

Sloth bear

Sun bear

Spectacled bear

Moon bear

American black bear

5

What do you eat?

I eat fish!

I am a type of brown bear called a grizzly. I stand by the river's edge and catch the fish that swim past me.

Bears mostly eat berries, roots, leaves, and fruits.

Yummy ants

Sun bears have very long tongues. They use them to lick up grubs, ants, and honey.

Hungry bear

Giant pandas eat bamboo, which is a type of tall grass that grows in China. Pandas need big, strong teeth to chew the bamboo.

Q. What is a polar bear's favorite fast food?

A. Ice burgers!

Activity time

Get ready to make and do!

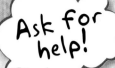

Ask for help!

Draw me!

YOU WILL NEED: pencils · paper

1. Draw a squashed circle. Add two rounded shapes for ears.

2. Now draw the body, small tail and two legs.

3. Add the eyes, nose and mouth, and draw two more legs.

Teddy bear picnic

Invite your friends and their teddies to a teddy bear picnic. Ask an adult to help you make a healthy one.

Now color me in and give me a name!

Paper bag bears

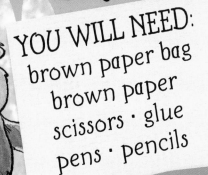

Ask for help!

YOU WILL NEED:
brown paper bag
brown paper
scissors · glue
pens · pencils

HERE'S HOW:
1. Fold the bottom corners of the bag to make a face shape.
2. Cut out two ears and two paws from the paper. Stick them on the bag.
3. Draw the bear's face.

If you have a white paper bag and black paper, try making a panda puppet.

Bear Oat Bars

YOU WILL NEED:
9 tbsp butter · ½ cup brown sugar
3 tbsp light corn syrup
2 tbsp molasses
1 cup rolled oats · ⅙ cup raisins
⅙ cup chopped nuts

HERE'S HOW:
1. Turn on oven to 350°F (180°C).
2. Gently heat the butter, sugar, molasses, and corn syrup in a saucepan.
3. Stir in the oats, raisins, and nuts.
4. Pour the mixture into an 8-inch (20 cm) square baking tin and squash it down a bit with a spoon.
5. Bake for 30 minutes. Then cut into squares and allow to cool before taking out of the tin.

Ask for help!

Where do you live?

I live in the forest.

There are mountains and rivers nearby.
I live here because there is lots of
food for my cubs.

Sleepy time

Females look after their cubs in dens, which are safe holes under trees or rocks. Bears rest in dens when it is cold outside.

Cold life

Polar bears live in the icy north. Their thick white coats keep them warm. They have huge paws that help them run across the slippery ice.

Q. Why do polar bears wear thick coats?

A. Because they'd look silly wearing woolly hats!

How fast can you run?

I can run very fast.

Even though I am a large, heavy animal, I can charge at over 30 miles (48 km) an hour!

Q. Have you ever hunted bear?
A. No, but I have been hunting with my clothes on!

Running

12

Swimming

In the water
Polar bears love to swim. They can hold their breath underwater for two minutes.

In the trees
Bears are good at climbing. They use their sharp claws to help them grip trees.

Climbing

LEARN A WORD:
charge
When one animal runs at another animal to attack it.

What are your babies called?

My babies are called cubs.

My cubs are just 6 inches (15 cm) long when they are born. I carry them gently in my mouth.

Giant panda

Piggyback

Sloth bear moms carry their cubs on their backs until they are about nine months old.

Growing up

Bear cubs love to play and pretend to fight. When they are old enough, they leave their mothers to find new homes of their own.

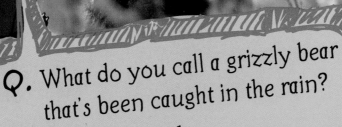

Q. What do you call a grizzly bear that's been caught in the rain?

A. A drizzly bear!

Puzzle time

Can you solve all the puzzles?

Berry Feast

Bryan the bear has five berries. One of his friends has three berries, and another friend has two. How many berries do the three bears have altogether?

ANSWER: Ten

True or false?

1. All bears have fur.
2. Polar bears live in warm forests.
3. A baby bear is called a kitten.

ANSWERS: 1. True 2. False 3. False

Tell us apart

There are three differences between Barney and Billy — can you spot them?

Barney

Billy

GROWL

Rhyme time

Only four of these words rhyme with "bear." Can you find them?

chair ear cub pear speak fair dairy furry hare den

ANSWER: chair pear fair hare

Who caught the fish?

Use your finger to trace each fishing line and discover which lucky bear caught the fish.

ANSWER: Belinda

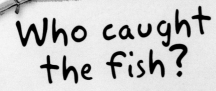

Bethany

Belinda

Bertha

What do you look like?

I have light fur around my eyes.

These eye markings make it look like I am wearing glasses!

Spectacled bear

Ghost bears
Some American black bears are born with white coats, which make them look like ghosts.

Moon marking
Moon bears have a large white mark on their chests, which looks like a crescent moon.

Q. What goes black, white, black, white, bump?
A. A panda rolling down a hill!

19

Are you scary?

All bears can be dangerous.

We have powerful muscles and are very strong. We also have large jaws, big teeth, and sharp claws.

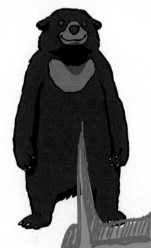

Q. Why wasn't the bear hungry?

A. Because he was stuffed.

People and bears

Most bears are shy animals and they are easily frightened. They prefer to stay away from people.

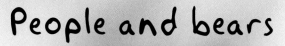

LEARN A WORD:
claw
An animal's large, sharp nails are called claws.

Deadly bears
Adult male polar bears will have fights. They stand tall and growl at each other.

Goldilocks and the Three Bears

Once upon a time, there was a little girl called Goldilocks. Her mother told her never to go off on her own, but one day, Goldilocks sneaked down a path that led into the forest. Soon she was lost. At last, she saw a light through the trees. It was coming from a cottage. She opened the door and went in.

On the table inside were three bowls of porridge. The big bowl was too tall for her to reach. The middle-sized bowl was too hot. But the little one was just right, so she ate it all up.

By the fire were three chairs. Goldilocks couldn't climb up onto the big chair. The middle-sized chair was too hard. The little chair was just the right size for her, but as soon as she sat down, it broke into pieces.

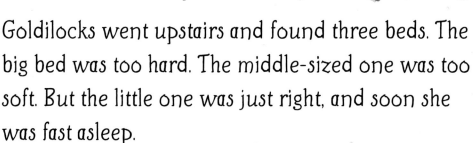

Goldilocks went upstairs and found three beds. The big bed was too hard. The middle-sized one was too soft. But the little one was just right, and soon she was fast asleep.

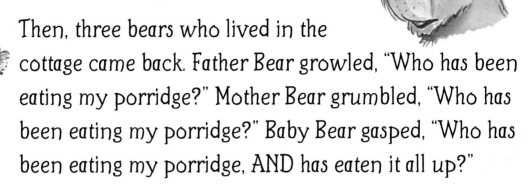

Then, three bears who lived in the cottage came back. Father Bear growled, "Who has been eating my porridge?" Mother Bear grumbled, "Who has been eating my porridge?" Baby Bear gasped, "Who has been eating my porridge, AND has eaten it all up?"

The bears saw the chairs. Father Bear growled, "Who has been sitting in my chair?" Mother Bear grumbled, "Who has been sitting in my chair?" Baby Bear gasped, "Who has been sitting in my chair, AND has broken it?"

The bears went upstairs. Father Bear growled, "Who has been sleeping in my bed?" Mother Bear grumbled, "Who has been sleeping in my bed?" Baby Bear gasped, "Who has been sleeping in my bed, AND is still there?"

Just then, Goldilocks woke up. She ran from the bears and out of the door. She found her way home and promised never to wander off again.

By Andrew Lang

Glossary

bamboo a type of tall grass that grows in China

cottage a small, simple house

crescent a curved shape, such as the moon when less than half of it is visible

den a wild animal's home, sometimes in a tree or cave

gasp to breathe in suddenly with the mouth open, out of pain or surprise

growl a deep sound made by an animal in a show of anger or unfriendliness

mammal animals, usually with hair or fur, that feed their young with milk

porridge oatmeal or cereal boiled in water or milk

powerful having great power or strength

spectacled wearing glasses or having markings that look like glasses

Index

Websites

For web resources related to the subject of this book, go to: **www.windmillbooks.com/weblinks** and select this book's title.